YOU CAN MASTER MATH!

Let's Have Fun with Shapes

By Mike Askew

PowerKiDS press
New York

Published in 2022 by The Rosen Publishing Group, Inc.
29 East 21st Street, New York, NY 10010

© Ruby Tuesday Books Limited 2020

All rights reserved. No part of this book may be reproduced in any form without permission in writing from the publisher, except by a reviewer.

Editors: Ruth Owen and Mark J. Sachner
Designer: Emma Randall

Images courtesy of Ruby Tuesday Books and Shutterstock.

Cataloging-in-Publication Data

Names: Askew, Mike.
Title: Let's have fun with shapes / Mike Askew.
Description: New York : PowerKids Press, 2022. | Series: You can master math!
Identifiers: ISBN 9781725331594 (pbk.) | ISBN 9781725331617 (library bound) | ISBN 9781725331600 (6 pack) | ISBN 9781725331624 (ebook)
Subjects: LCSH: Shapes--Juvenile literature.
Classification: LCC QA445.5 A85 2022 | DDC 516'.15--dc23

Manufactured in the United States of America

CPSIA Compliance Information: Batch #CSPK22
For Further Information contact Rosen Publishing, New York, New York at 1-800-237-993

Circle
Equilateral triangle
Scalene triangle
Square
Rectangle
Pentagon

Contents

Line Designs 4
Shape Hunt 5
Take 4 Triangles 6
Two-Piece Tangram 7
Follow My Lead 8
Fill the Grid 10
Midpoint Patterns 11
Exploded Square 12
Exploring Symmetry 14
Birthday Card Jigsaw 16
Build a Box 17
What's My Shape? 18
Square & Triangle Challenge 20
3D Skeleton Shapes 22
Paper Patterns 24
Gnome Homes 25
Flying Fish 26
Curve Stitching 27
Let's Play Buried Treasure 28

Tips for Math Success 30

Hexagon Octagon Trapezoid 5-point star 6-point star

Line Designs

Get Ready

You will need:
- A sheet of paper
- A ruler
- A pencil
- Colored pens or pencils

Use your ruler and pencil to draw straight lines on the paper.

Put the lines in different places and make them cross each other to make a pattern.

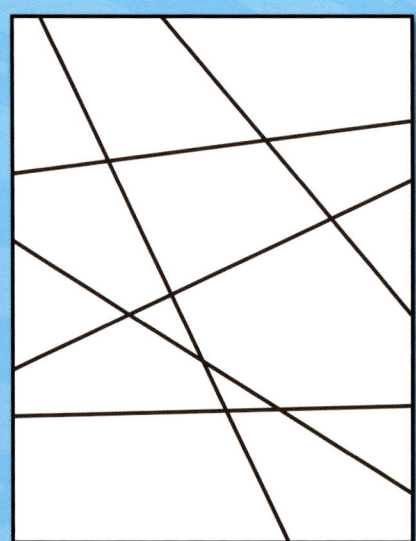

Keep drawing lines until you are happy with your pattern.

1 Look at your pattern.

Can you find any shapes with 3 sides?

If you can, color them all in with the same color.

2 Next, can you see any shapes with 4 sides?

If you can, color them all in with a different color.

Draw another pattern that has 3-, 4-, 5-, 6-, and 8-sided shapes.

3 Keep going! Look for shapes with 5 sides, 6 sides, and so on. Color each group in a different color.

4

Shape Hunt

Get Ready

You will need:
- A ruler
- A pencil or pen
- Paper

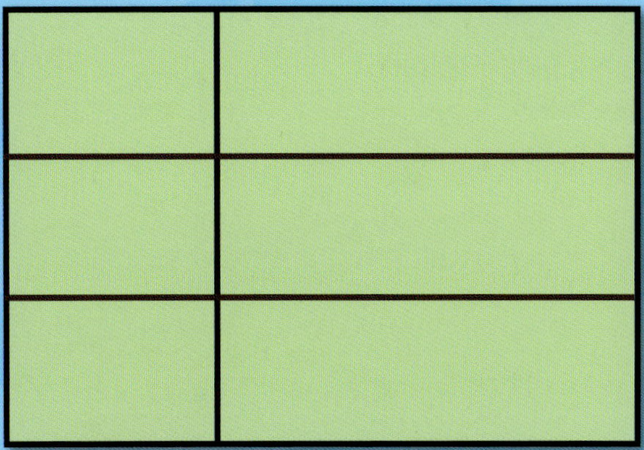

Look at the rectangle.

How many rectangles can you find within the big rectangle?

I think there are 6 rectangles.

I think there are more than 6 rectangles.

Now look at this triangle.

How many triangles can you find within the big triangle?

Go For It!

Use your ruler, pencil, and paper to make up a puzzle like these and challenge a friend to solve it!

Take 4 Triangles

Get Ready

You will need:
- 2 squares of thick paper, about 6 inches x 6 inches (15 cm x 15 cm)
- A pencil or pen
- Ruler
- Scissors

Take your two squares and draw a line from corner to corner.

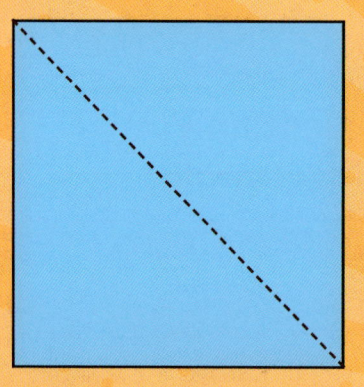
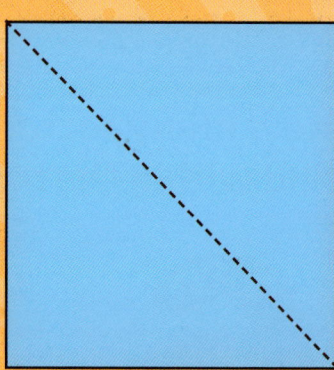

Carefully cut along the lines to make four triangles.

Now try fitting your triangles back together again to make other shapes.

Can you make these shapes?
- A big triangle
- A square
- A rectangle
- A pentagon (a shape with five sides)
- A hexagon (a shape with six sides)
- An octagon (a shape with eight sides)

Four's Fantastic Facts

The line from corner to corner on your squares is called a **diagonal**.

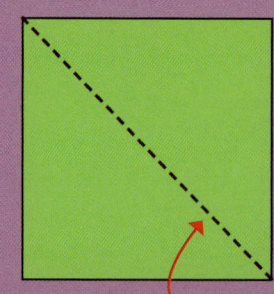
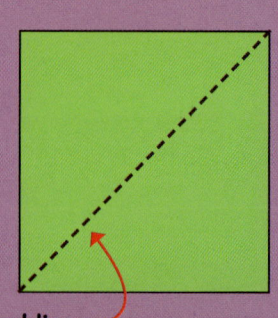

Diagonal lines

Two-Piece Tangram

Get Ready

You will need:
- A square of thick paper, about 6 inches x 6 inches (15 cm x 15 cm)
- A pencil or pen
- Ruler
- Scissors

Find the middle point on one side of your square. You can do this by measuring with a ruler.

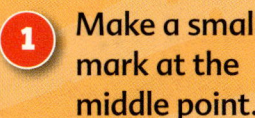

1 Make a small mark at the middle point.

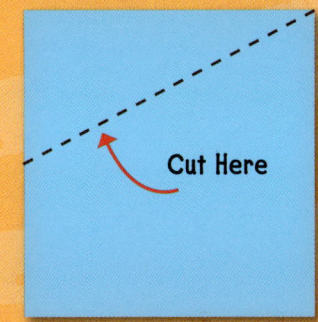

2 Use your ruler to draw a line from the middle point to the opposite corner.

3 Then cut along this line to make a triangle and a four-sided shape.

Which of these shapes can you make with your two pieces?
- A big triangle
- A rectangle
- A pentagon
- A hexagon
- An octagon

Four's Fantastic Facts

Some of the most famous square-shaped puzzles are called tangrams. A tangram has seven pieces and might look like this.

Follow My Lead

Get Ready

You will need:
- A collection of small shapes (two of everything)
- A large book (to stand up as a screen)
- A friend to play with

You can make the shapes to play "Follow My Lead" by cutting them from paper or cardboard. Make sure you have two of everything.

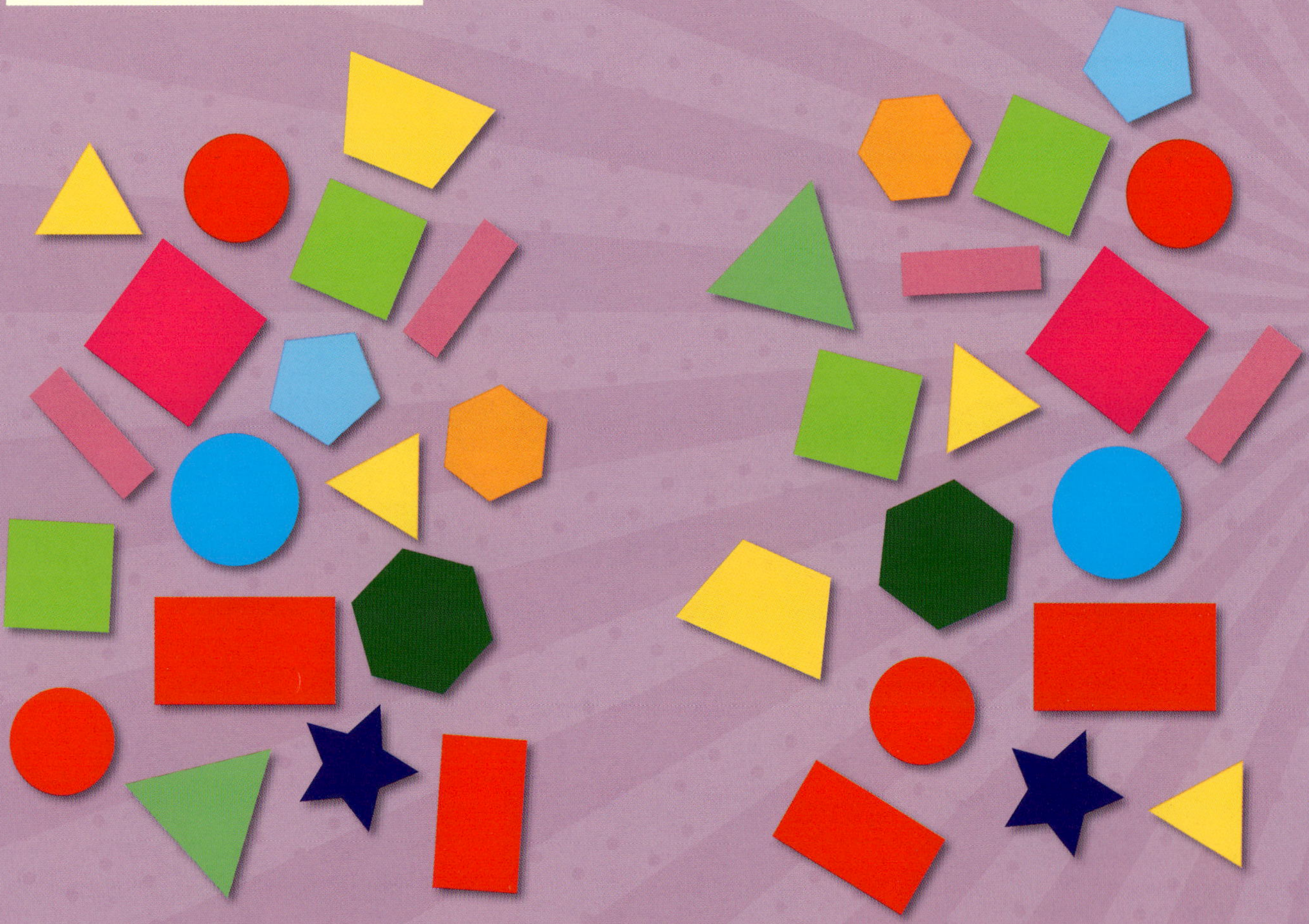

 You can ask an adult to help you find patterns for shapes online. They can help you download and print shapes to cut out.

① Stand up the book to make a screen between you and your friend.

② Make a design with your shapes behind the screen. Make sure your friend can't see your picture.

③ Now you must give your friend instructions so they can make your design on their side of the screen.

For example, you might say, "Put a green triangle above a blue circle."

④ When your friend thinks they have made your design, take away the screen to check.

Your friend's picture

Your picture

Your friend can ask you questions if they are not sure what to do.

The better your instructions are, the closer your two pictures should match!

⑤ Take turns. Now your friend makes a design and you must follow their instructions.

9

Fill the Grid

Get Ready

You will need:
- Paper
- Scissors
- A red, blue, and yellow pen or pencil

Cut nine little squares from some paper. The squares should be the same size as the squares on the grid below.

To fill the grid, you must draw each of the three shapes in the three colors.

For example, take one of the little squares you cut out. Draw a triangle on the square and color it red.

Now place the red triangle on the correct square on the grid. We've done this one for you!

Now, try to fill in the rest of the grid!

Try making up and drawing your own grid of shapes and colors.

Midpoint Patterns

Get Ready

You will need:
- Paper
- A ruler
- Colored pens or pencils

1 Use your ruler to draw a triangle.

2 Now make a small mark in about the middle of each side of the triangle.

3 Join the marks together. You've made another triangle!

4 Now repeat Steps 2 and 3 on the new triangle.

What do you notice?

Keep going! You can color in your pattern, too.

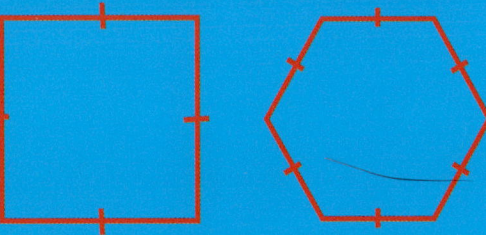

Now try doing this but start with a four-sided shape.

What happens if you try with a six-sided shape?

11

Exploded Square

Follow the instructions to make your exploded square picture.

Get Ready

You will need:
- A square of colored paper, 6 inches by 6 inches (15x15 cm)
- Scissors
- A sheet of white paper
- A glue stick

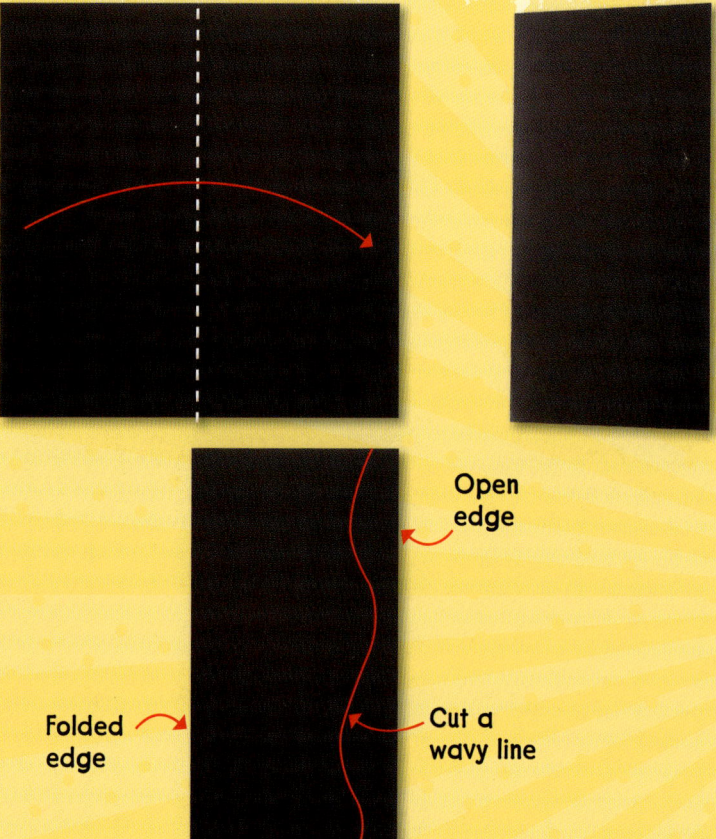

1 Fold the square of paper in half.

2 Now carefully cut a strip off the edge of the paper. You should be cutting along the open edges, not the folded edge.

Make your cut wavy and interesting and make sure you are cutting through both sides of the paper.

Open edge

Folded edge

Cut a wavy line

3 Now cut off another wavy strip. Again, make sure you are cutting through both sides of the paper.

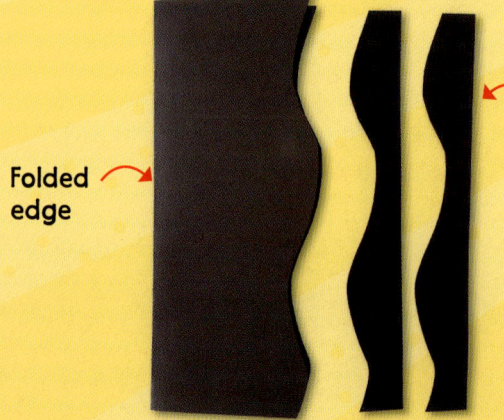

Folded edge

Pieces cut from the edge of the paper

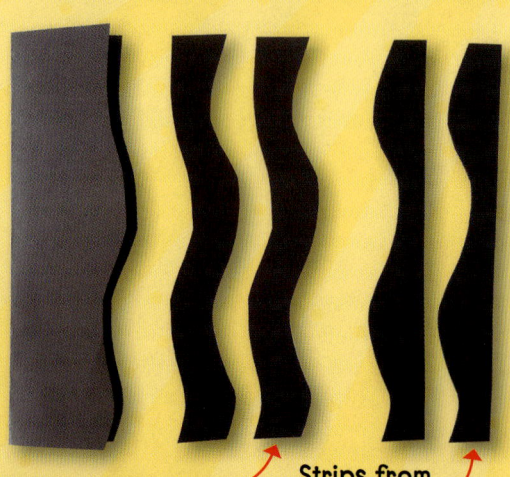

Strips from second cut

Strips from first cut

12

4 Finally, cut off another wavy strip.

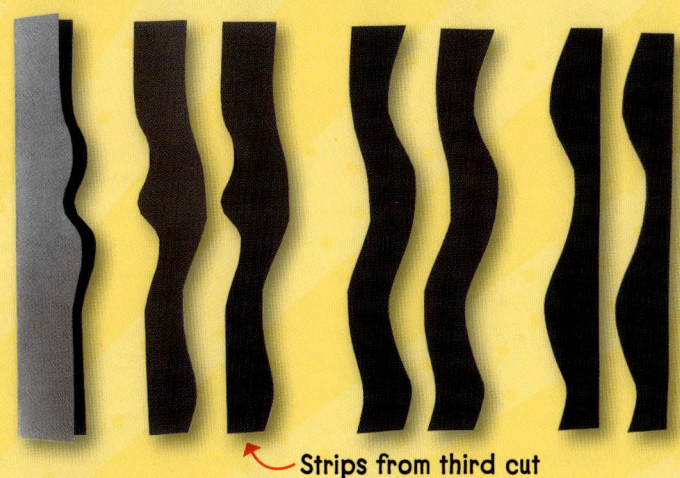

Strips from third cut

5 Unfold the creased piece of paper. Stick it onto the middle of your white piece of paper.

6 Now find the two strips that fit with the creased piece of paper. Glue the strips next to the middle piece, but leave a gap.

7 Find the next two pieces that match up with the edges of the pattern, and glue them onto the white paper.

Four's Fantastic Facts

A shape, design, or picture like this, where one side exactly matches the other, is called **symmetrical**.

8 Finally, glue the last two strips in place. Your exploded square is complete!

13

Exploring Symmetry

Get Ready

You will need:
- An old magazine (check with an adult that it's OK to cut up the magazine)
- Scissors
- A sheet of paper
- A glue stick
- Colored pens or pencils

Face Match

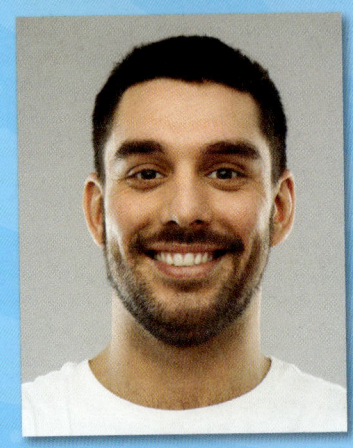

Find a picture of a face in a magazine. Look for a picture where the person is looking straight at you.

1 Cut out the picture. Then cut the face in half from top to bottom.

2 Glue half of the face onto the sheet of paper.

3 Use colored pens and pencils to draw in the other half of the face.

14

Butterfly Match

Get Ready

You will need:
- A square of colored paper
- A pencil
- Scissors
- Paints

Take your square of paper and fold it in half.

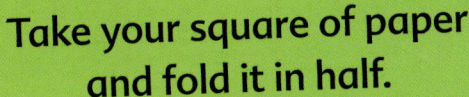

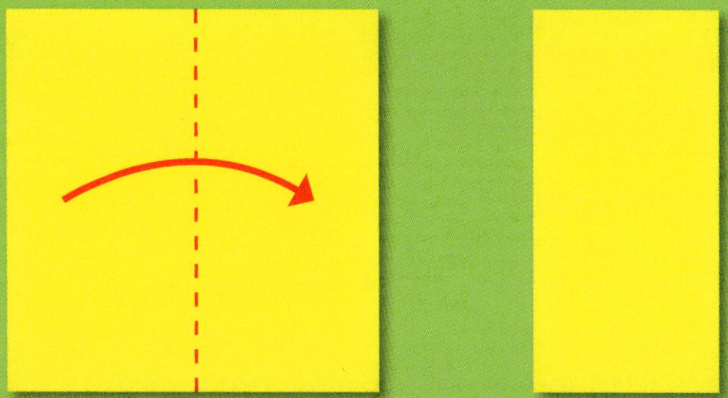

1. Draw half a butterfly on the folded paper.

Make sure the butterfly's body is against the fold.

2. Carefully cut around the outline of the butterfly and open it up.

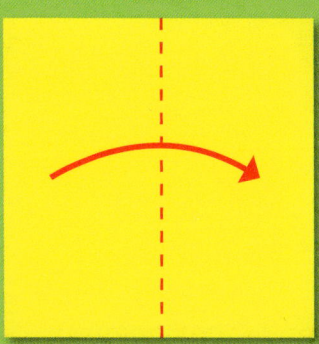

3. Put some blobs of paint on one half of your butterfly.

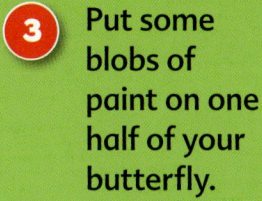

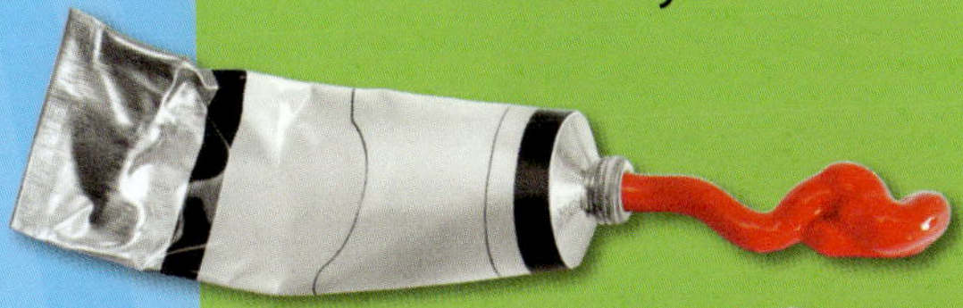

4. Fold the butterfly closed again and rub over the outside to transfer paint onto the other half.

5. Open up your beautiful symmetrical butterfly.

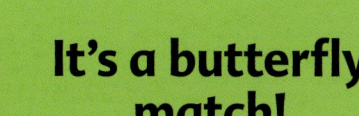

It's a butterfly match!

Birthday Card Jigsaw

Get Ready

You will need:
- The front of an old birthday card
- Scissors
- A friend to play with

Use an old birthday card to make this fun jigsaw game.

1. Cut up the front of the birthday card into nine pieces. Make each piece an interesting shape.

2. Mix up the pieces and lay them faceup on the table.

3. Now, your job is to help your friend put the picture back together, like a jigsaw puzzle. You must give your friend instructions using shape, position, and orientation words.

For example, you could say, "Pick up the rectangle with the giraffe's face. Put it in the top right-hand corner of the picture. Turn it clockwise so it is the right way up."

You must not touch any of the pieces!

Build a Box

Get Ready

You will need:
- An empty cereal box
- Scissors
- Masking tape or low-stick tape
- Paper and a pencil or pen
- An adult helper

1 Ask an adult to help you cut the cereal box into sections. Only cut along the edges.

You should now have 6 rectangles.

(See further instructions regarding cutting up the box on page 31.)

2 Now use tape to stick the 6 pieces back together. You need to make a flat shape that will fold up to remake the box.

Draw what your flat shape looks like.

3 Carefully peel off the tape.

Can you find a different way to join the 6 rectangles so that they still fold up to make the box?

Draw this arrangement, too.

How many different ways can you find to remake the box?

Four's Fantastic Facts

A flat shape that folds up to make a box is called a **net**.

17

Know Your Shapes

Square

Rectangle

Circle

Trapezoid

Pentagon

Hexagon

Equilateral triangle

Scalene triangle

5-point star

6-point star

What's My Shape?

Get Ready

You will need:
- Lots of counters
- A friend to play with
- Paper and pens or pencils

1. Each player takes a big handful of counters and chooses one of the boards on page 19. Decide who goes first. They are Player One.

2. Next, each player chooses a shape from their board and writes down their choice, keeping it hidden from their opponent. For example:
   Pentagon/Big/Blue   6-pointed star/Small/Red

3. Each player must now guess their opponent's chosen shape by taking turns asking questions.

4. Player One starts and asks Player Two a question about their shape. For example: **"Is your shape green?"**

   If the answer is **"No,"** Player Two uses counters to cover up all the green shapes on their board that have now been eliminated. If the answer is **"Yes,"** Player Two covers all the red, blue, orange, yellow and pink shapes.

5. Then it is Player Two's turn to ask a question.

6. Keep taking turns until one player can guess their opponent's shape and win the game!

Here's an example of game play:
Player One: *Is your shape green?*
Player Two: *No*
Player Two covers all the green shapes on their board.
Player Two: *Does your shape have four sides?*
Player One: *Yes*
Player One covers all the shapes on their board that don't have four sides.
Player One: *Is your shape big?*
Player Two: *No*
Player Two covers all the big shapes on their board.

18

Player sits here

Board B

Board A

Player sits here

19

Square & Triangle Challenge

Get Ready

You will need:
- 20 toothpicks or pencils that are exactly the same length

Making Squares

These squares have been made using 12 pencils.

Can you see five squares?

Now it's your turn. Take 20 pencils or toothpicks.

What is the biggest number of squares you can make by putting them together?

If you're using toothpicks, you're not allowed to bend or break them.

Growing Triangle

Here are 3 pencils making a triangle.

Here is the next size triangle. It takes 6 pencils to make this triangle.

How many pencils do you think you will need to make the next size triangle?

Check your prediction by making the triangle.

How about the next size up?

Go For It!

This square has been made with 4 pencils.

How many pencils will you need to make the next size square?

21

3D Skeleton Shapes

Get Ready

You will need:
- Toothpicks
- Modeling clay

Skeleton shapes are not spooky. They are just shapes made from toothpicks and modeling clay!

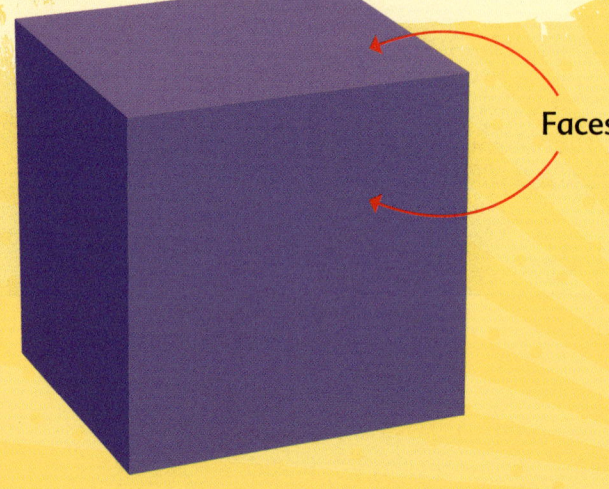
Faces

This is a cube. A cube is a solid, or **three-dimensional (3D)**, shape.

The sides of the cube are called **faces**.

This is the skeleton of a cube.

Take some toothpicks and modeling clay and make your own skeleton cube.

How many toothpicks are needed?

How many balls of modeling clay?

Four's Fantastic Facts

The parts of the skeleton created by the toothpicks are the **edges** of the shape.

The places where there are balls of modeling clay are the **vertices**.

22

Paper Patterns

Have fun with this activity folding, predicting, and cutting.

Get Ready

You will need:
- Lots of squares of paper (you can use scrap paper or paper that's been written on)
- Scissors
- Paper and a pen or pencil

1 Take a square of paper and fold it in half.

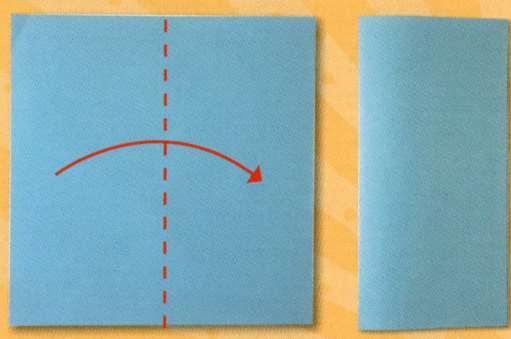

2 Next, fold the paper in half again.

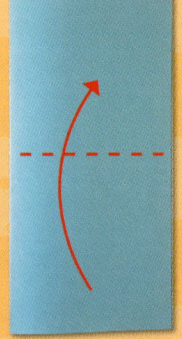

3 Now you are going to cut off the corner of the paper like this.

4 Before you open the paper, draw a sketch of the shape you think you will see when you unfold the paper.

5 Now, open up the folds.

Was your sketch correct?

6 Take another square of paper. Make the same two folds as before. Then make a third fold.

What shape do you think will be made when you cut off the point?

Draw a sketch of your prediction. Make the cut and open up the folds.

GO For It!

Can you find a way to fold and cut your paper to make a 6-sided shape?

How about an 8-pointed star?

Gnome Homes

Get Ready

You will need:
• Modeling clay

Gnomes live in homes made out of exactly four cubes.

Gnomes build their houses by joining the faces, or sides, of cubes exactly.

This is a gnome home.

This is not.

Gnomes like their houses to be only one story high. They do not stack cubes on top of each other.

So this is a gnome home.

But this is not.

Try building some gnome homes out of modeling clay.

Try building some bigger gnome homes using five cubes.

Your cubes don't have to be big. About the size of large dice is perfect.

How many different gnome homes can you make?

25

Flying Fish

Get Ready

You will need:
- A cardboard square, 4 x 4 inches (10 x 10 cm)
- Scissors
- Sticky tape
- A large sheet of paper
- Colored pencils or pens

Try making a series of fish shapes that fit together.

1 Draw a line from one side of the square of cardboard to the opposite side.

Make the line look a little like the head of a fish.

2 Cut along the line to make two pieces.

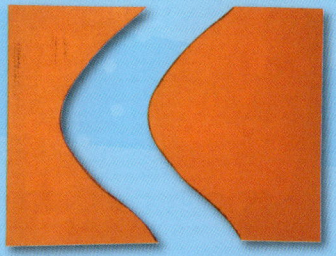

3 Now swap the positions of the two pieces and join them with sticky tape.

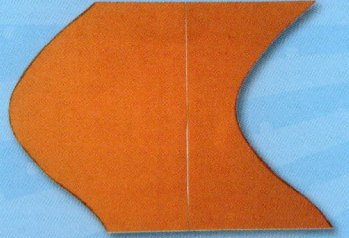

4 Now lay your cardboard fish shape on the large piece of paper. Draw around the shape.

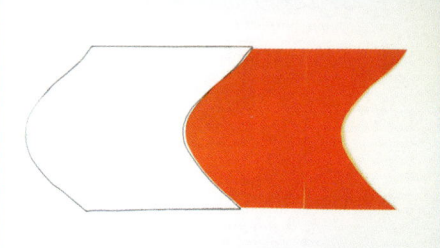

Then move the shape to a new position so it fits exactly with the fish outline you've just drawn.

5 Keep drawing around the cardboard shape to make lots of outlines that all fit together.

Decorate your flying fish!

Four's Fantastic Facts

Shapes that fit together like this are called tessellating shapes. A famous artist named M. C. Escher made lots of pictures like this.

Can you see the lizards in this tessellation pattern?

26

Curve Stitching

Get Ready

You will need:
- A sheet of paper
- A ruler
- Colored pens or pencils

Draw two lines on your sheet of paper.

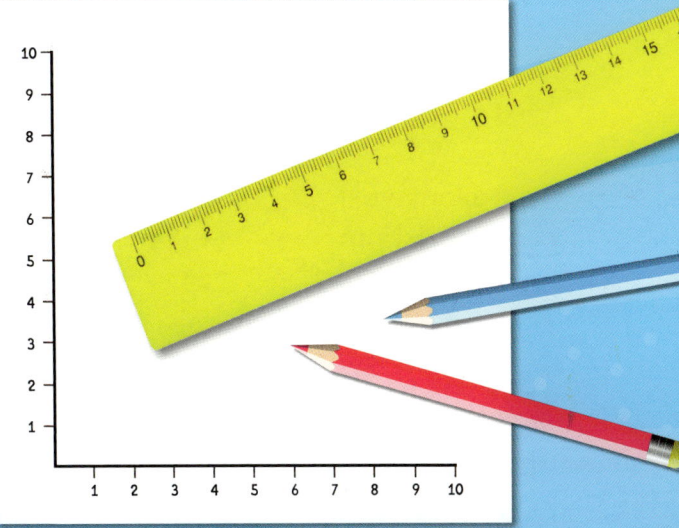

Each line should be 10 centimeters long. That's about 4 inches.

Mark each centimeter on the two lines and number the marks from 1 to 10.

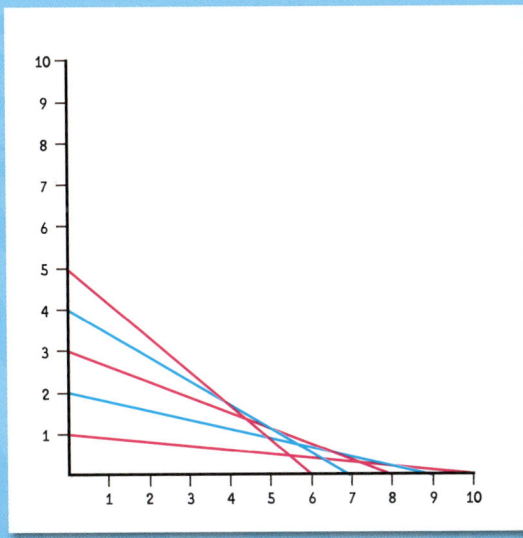

Now begin joining the points on each line that add up to eleven.

Use your ruler and a pen or pencil to join 1 to 10, 2 to 9, 3 to 8, and so on.

What do you notice about the colored lines?

Go For It!

Now, draw a square that's 10 centimeters x 10 centimeters. Mark each centimeter on the four sides of the square. Then start joining the pairs of numbers that add up to eleven. Can you make a curve in every corner of your square?

Let's Play Buried Treasure

Get ready to hunt for buried treasure on a desert island!

Get Ready

You will need:
- Counters or buttons
- A book to stand up as a screen
- Paper and pens or pencils (for recording guesses)
- A friend to play with

1. Each player chooses to play on one of the boards on page 29.

2. Stand a book between the two boards, like a screen, so the players can't see their opponent's board.

3. Each player puts four pieces of treasure (counters) on four different squares on their board.

4. Now the players must take turns to guess where their opponent's treasure is buried. For example:

    Player One: "Is there treasure in square A3?"

    If A3 is correct, Player Two says **"Green"** and gives Player One the treasure.

    If A3 is one square away from treasure, Player Two says **"Orange."**

    If the guess is any other square, Player Two says **"Red."**

5. Now it's Player Two's turn to pick a square, and Player One must say whether it's Green, Orange, or Red.

6. The winner is the first player to collect all their opponent's treasure!

Can you find a way to record your guesses to help you find the treasure?

Player 1
A B C D E F
1 2 3 4 5 6

6 5 4 3 2 1
A B C D E F
Player 2

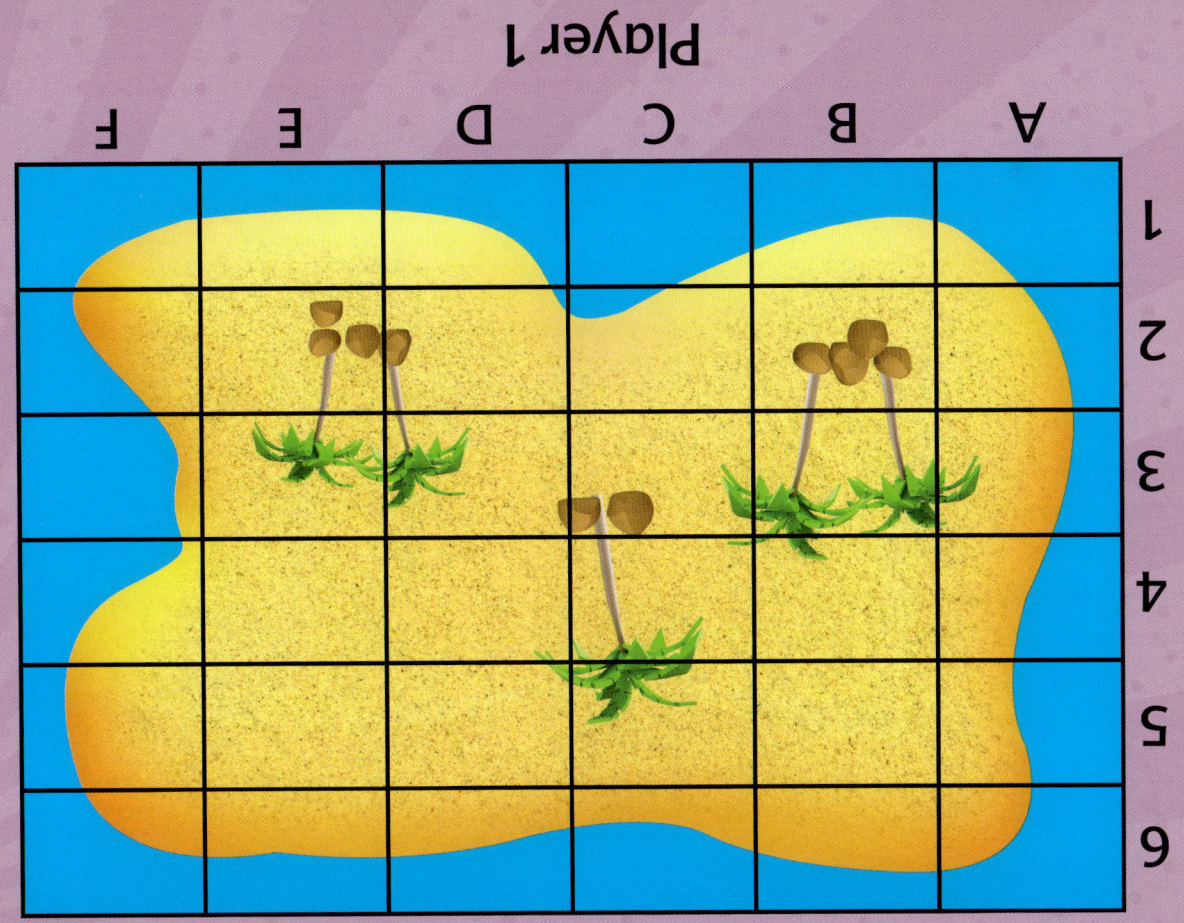

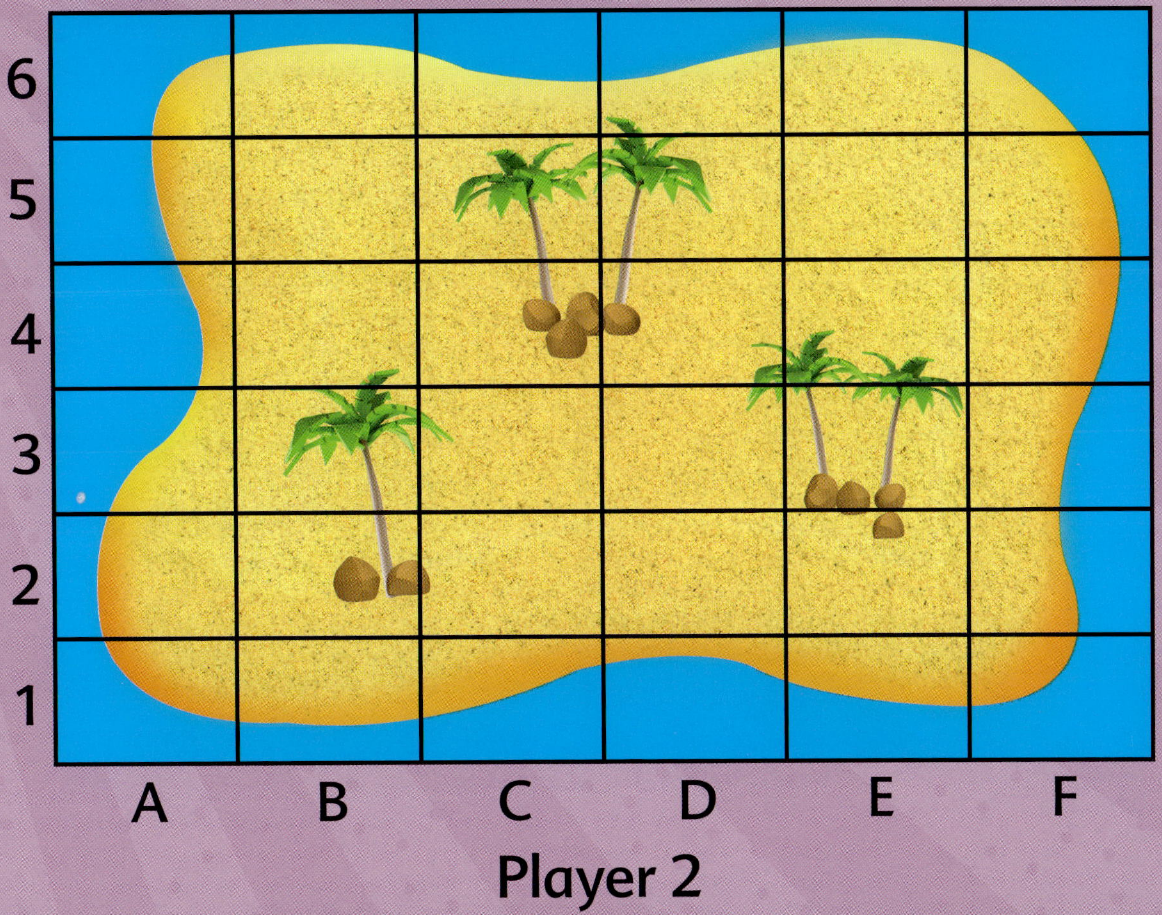

Tips for Math Success

Page 4: Line Designs

This activity will help learners explore the different two-dimensional shapes that can be made from straight lines. Once they have colored some of the shapes, you can talk about the names that we give shapes.

Page 5: Shape Hunt

Being able to see shapes within other shapes is a skill that will help learners in lots of future mathematics. There are 17 rectangles to be found (including the big one) and 8 triangles (including the big one).

Page 6: Take 4 Triangles

The four triangles can be used to make:

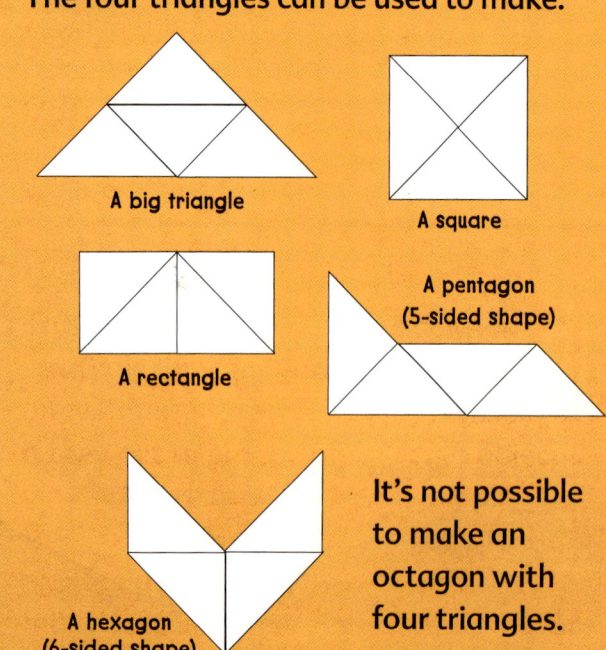

It's not possible to make an octagon with four triangles.

Page 7: Two-Piece Tangram

A two-piece tangram can be used to make the following shapes:

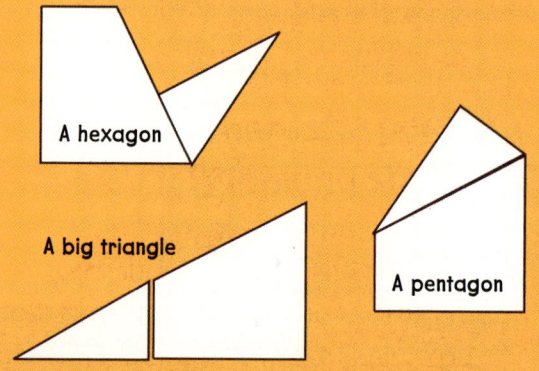

It's not possible to make a rectangle or octagon from the tangram.

Pages 8—9: Follow My Lead

This activity will help learners refine three key aspects of the language of shape and space: describing shapes *(take the small green square)*, orientation *(turn it so that it looks like a diamond)*, and position *(put it to the right-hand side of the circle)*.

Page 10: Fill the Grid

Coordinating two properties — in this case color and shape — is another skill that will be helpful and useful to learners. Once they have filled the grid, you could play "what's my shape?" Take turns thinking of one of the nine shapes, and the other player has to figure out what it is by asking questions that only have a YES or NO answer.

Page 11: Midpoint Patterns

It's fine to guess the midpoints of the sides of the shapes. But if learners are ready to use a ruler, show them how to use it to measure the sides of the shapes and to halve that length to mark the midpoints accurately.

Pages 12—13: Exploded Square

Some scientists think that we are born with an innate sense of symmetry. This activity and the projects on pages 14 and 15 will help learners refine that sense. Exploded Square is a great introduction to the concept of symmetry. The pattern can be as simple or intricate as they like, but they will soon see that both sides will always be symmetrical.

Pages 14—15: Exploring Symmetry

If you have a color printer, it's fun to look at the symmetry of the learner's face. Take a photo of them and print it out. Then flip the image and print that version (so you have a mirror image of the original picture).

 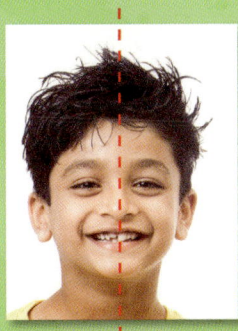

Cut each picture in half and then make two new faces from the two left sides and the two right sides.

Each new face will be perfectly symmetrical. Which face do learners like best?

Page 16: Birthday Card Jigsaw

If you're playing with learners, it can be helpful to "play dumb." You might know what the learner means, but if their instruction is not completely clear, then playfully get it wrong. For example, if they say, "Put that piece by the first piece," put it above the first piece, even though you know they meant for it to be placed at the side. When you get the instruction wrong, they will have to think again about the words they are using and make their instruction clearer.

Page 17: Build a Box

You may need to do a little advance preparation here. Many cereal boxes have two flaps that connect to make the lid. Cut one of these flaps off and tape it to the other so that there are six rectangles when the box is cut apart.

Pages 18—19: What's My Shape?

This fun guessing game requires logic. You might need to help learners appreciate the power of negative answers. For example, there might only

31

Pages 18—19: continued

be squares and circles left on the board. "Is it a square?" the learner asks. You answer, "No." Rather than realizing that this means it must be a circle, they may think getting the answer wrong is not helpful and go on to ask, "Is it a circle?"

Pages 20—21: Square & Triangle Challenge

You can make 9 squares with 20 pencils. Here are two ways:

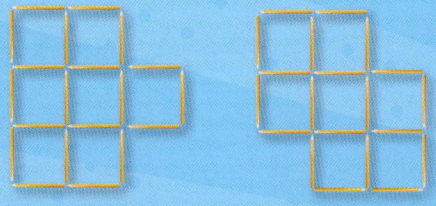

Here is the growing triangle and square.

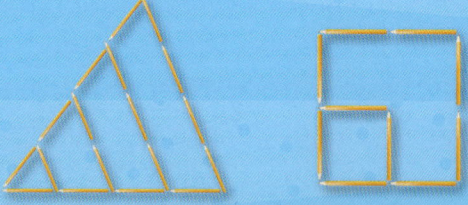

Pages 22—23: 3D Skeleton Shapes

While making the skeleton shapes, talk about the number of corners and edges the 3D skeletons have and encourage learners to visualize the sides being filled in to count the number of faces. You can make a tetrahedron with 6 sticks and 4 balls of modeling clay.

Page 24: Paper Patterns

Visualizing (picturing shapes in your head) is important when working with shapes and space. This activity will engage learners in visualizing. If you do it together, talk about what you think the shape is going to be and how you are figuring that out before unfolding it. You can also explore how many different ways the cut-out piece can be fitted back into the hole in the square of paper.

Page 25: Gnome Homes

When investigating which gnome home shapes are possible, talk about what counts as different. Ask, "Are these two houses the same or different?" There is no correct answer. The important thing is for learners to come up with reasons for why the shapes are different or are not.

Page 26: Flying Fish

Look up the work of M. C. Escher online. Learners may be inspired to make some more detailed tessellations.

Page 27: Curve Stitching

There is something magical about the way a curve emerges out of drawing straight lines. A square with a curve in each corner should look like this.

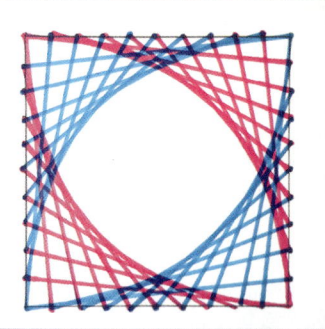

Pages 28—29: Let's Play Buried Treasure

This game will introduce learners to coordinates. The convention is to go along first and then up, so encourage learners to say B2 rather than 2B.